Take Care of Yourself

Staying Safe from Injuries

by Mari Schuh

Raintree is an imprint of Capstone Global Library Limited, a company incorporated in England and Wales having its registered office at 264 Banbury Road, Oxford, OX2 7DY – Registered company number: 6695582

www.raintree.co.uk
myorders@raintree.co.uk

Edited by Erika L. Shores
Designed by Heidi Thompson
Media research by Jo Miller
Original illustrations © Capstone Global Library Limited 2023
Originated by Capstone Global Library Ltd
Production by Tori Abraham
Printed and bound in India

978 1 3982 4212 8 (hardback)
978 1 3982 4213 5 (paperback)

British Library Cataloguing in Publication Data
A full catalogue record for this book is available from the British Library.

Acknowledgements
We would like to thank the following for permission to reproduce photographs: Capstone Studio: Karon Dubke, 8, 9, 11, 15; Getty Images: John D. Buffington, 18, Thomas Barwick, 10; Shutterstock: Anna Golant (design element) throughout, Anutr Yossundara, 5, Creativa Images, 14, Daniil Demin, 20, FOTOGRIN, 21, goodluz, cover, LightField Studios, 7, New Africa, 19, sirtravelalot, 13, Suzanne Tucker, 17

Contents

Staying safe 4

Take your time 6

On the move. 8

Play time 10

Cuts and scrapes 12

Staying safe from fire 14

Being safe around water 16

Fun in the sun 18

Your safety gear. 20

Glossary. 22

Find out more 23

Index. 24

About the author 24

Words in **bold** are in the glossary.

Staying safe

Everyone likes to have fun. But it's also important to be safe. Be aware of what is around you. Be mindful of what you are doing. When you are **prepared**, you can stay safe. You can keep yourself from being **injured**. And you can have lots of fun!

Take your time

Everyone gets busy! Remember to take your time doing things. You might get hurt if you rush. Don't run on ice or on wet areas. You might slip and fall. Walk slowly.

Take your time when you fill your school bag. Pack only the things you need. Make sure your school bag is not too heavy. Then you won't get hurt when you carry it.

On the move

Stay safe when you travel. When you go in a car, use a seat belt. When you take the bus, sit in your seat. Wait for the bus to stop. Then you can stand up.

Pay **attention** when you cross the road. Stop walking. Look and listen for moving cars and other **traffic**. Look left. Then look right. Look left again. Cross the street when no cars are moving.

Play time

It's fun to play sport! Make sure you have the equipment you need to be safe. A helmet can protect your head. You might wear shin pads in football.

Warm up before you play. Swing your
arms. Walk on the spot. Learn the rules of the
game. When you've finished, gently stretch
your body. It feels good!

Cuts and scrapes

Ouch! You might get a cut or scrape on your skin. You might get an insect bite. Clean your skin with soap and water. Let your skin dry. An adult can help you.

Put **antiseptic cream** on a clean plaster. Then put the plaster on the cut. This will stop the cut from getting **infected**. A **scab** might form over the cut. Don't pick it! It is helping your skin heal.

Staying safe from fire

Fire helps us cook. Fire keeps us warm. But fire can be dangerous. Stay away from matches, candles and fireworks. Don't touch hot cookers. Ask an adult to help you in the kitchen.

Practise fire drills at home and school. Practise staying low to avoid smoke. Plan an **escape route**. You can go to a safe place outside. If there's a fire, call 999. Always tell an adult.

Being safe around water

Splash, splash! You can learn to swim. Take swimming lessons. You will learn and have fun. Always swim with someone else. Never swim alone.

Be safe at a lake or river. Wear a life jacket. It helps you float. Wear it when you are in or near water. A life jacket helps keep you safe.

Fun in the sun

Everyone loves sunshine. But too much sun can harm your skin. You might get a **sunburn**. Put on suncream about 30 minutes before you go outside. After two hours, put on suncream again.

Protect your face and eyes. Wear
a hat and sunglasses. Take a sun break.
Find an area with shade. You can be
safe and have lots of fun!

Your safety gear

Safety gear is important. It can also be a fun way to show your style. Try this activity to make your gear your own.

What you need:

- your safety gear, such as your bike helmet or shin guards
- stickers
- colourful tape
- reflective tape

What you do:

1. Add your favourite stickers to your safety gear. How many stickers will you add? Have fun with it!

2. Now add some colourful tape. This will make your gear look different from other people's gear. What colours will you use?

3. Add strips of reflective tape. This will help people see you better. This can make you safer while you play.

Index

bus safety 8

crossing streets 9

fire safety 14, 15

helmets 10

injuries 4, 6, 12

mouth guards 10

plasters 12

school bags 6

seat belts 8

skin 12, 18

stretching 11

sun safety 18, 19

swimming 16

walking 6, 9, 11

water safety 16

About the author

Mari Schuh's love of reading began with cereal boxes at the kitchen table! Today, she is the author of hundreds of non-fiction books for early readers. Mari lives in the United States with her husband and their lively house rabbit. Learn more about her at marischuh.com.